# Written Words

## Ed Cross

**Back Cover Photograph**
**by**
**Guadalupe Laiz**

Editing Services by LINELLE

**ISBN-13: 978-1539772729**
**ISBN-10: 1539772721**

# CONTENTS

\* \* \* \* \*

# Afternoon in the Park

Warm sun, soft breeze
A wisp of cloud
The breath of flowers
Swaying, softly.
A scream of tires
Rubber burning
Traffic moving
Children playing
Running, hair bouncing free
Their silent will
To do, to be
To run and play under the summer sun
Seek and find
Thrill, have fun
'Til nightfall comes
Nature's shroud
And steals away the summer cloud
Then while children sleep
Perhaps their elders weep
Remembering
Those happy days gone by.

\* \* \* \* \*

# Appreciation

My enemies
Would have you believe
That I
Am a thief
That I stole from you
My friends
And neighbors
But it is they
Who have stolen
They have stolen my sleep
And they have tried
To steal
Those things of me
That I love
My integrity
My honesty
My dignity
This I will not allow
And in truth
Those enemies
Cannot succeed
I have served you well
For many years
For one reward
To be appreciated.
And now
My enemies
Would steal
That
Which in truth
They can only
Steal
From you.
* * * * *

## Aspen Day

Gray sky, no wind, brisk and clear
Eight new inches; no need for fear
The snow, deep and soft,
Waiting; a virgin bride
The quiet calm of the chairlift ride
The day begins
And now down the mountain, turning
The snow billowing, churning
Chest high, in the quiet of the trees
The only sound
The carving of your skis
Left and right, and always down
Diving, driving
Seeking, experiencing
The closeness of nature.
Such is why
I ski to live
And live to ski.

\* \* \* \* \*

# Aspen Mountain

**Aspen Mountain**
**Grand Old Lady**
**Regal**
**Silver Queen**
**Rugged, yet serene**
**A special hill**
**I've seen you kill**
**And maim and cripple**
**A luckless few**
**And pleasure many**
**with your supple curves**
**Majesty deserves**
**Respect**
**And should be given**
**Graciously**
**Lest it be**
**Demanded**

\* \* \* \* \*

## Avalanche

Why do we hope?
Why does the avalanche run?
What can we be
To seek, have fun?
Lose friends; watch one weep?
Over a soul, was never his to keep
Nor mine, or hers.
As I see it
Was as if she took a fit
Which wasn't her.
Angry or otherwise
Agitated.
I believe it was something fated
Or at least in God's mind
In any case
Was fate unkind?
Mita lived for life
And love
And snow
What we reap
Is what we sow.

\* \* \* \* \*

# Best of the Best

Sitting here,
Had a beer
And a margarita
Nothing sweeter
Than this, Sheer bliss
A great day
In a great life
'Cept for a wife,
Or two
Tho' that's not fair
They did their share
And then some
With my sons
And my daughter
All great kids
Along with Abby
Our half step sister
Always missed her
Maybe coming,
Back this way
Hope she'll stay
in Boulder
with Logan Fair
"Dinkum"
I'd love that

Love 'em all
And Hayley,
Can't forget Hayley,
Tyson's bride
After last year's
Wedding date
More than great
Wedding day
By the river,
in Colorado
And now
On the beach,
On "campus"
At Justin's house
"Grouse"!
An Aussie term
"Grouse"
The fair dinkum
Best there is
Like my kids
Best
Of the Best.

\* \* \* \* \*

## Black Shit Woman

Observation
I just spoke with a girl
Another bitch
By breeding
Or whatever.
Have you ever known a good woman?
I love my mother
But she's a bitch
Life's more
Than being rich
Or poor
Married, pregnant, chaste or sore
What you get
You pay the price for
I've paid
And never known
Other than the loving moan
Of woman
Never fully grown
Taking
What's hers to own
They take and cry
Men fight and die
Believing
They met a woman
with soul.
All I've met
Had hearts of coal
Black as shit.

\* \* \* \* \*

# Bonnie's

**Winter**
**Skiing**
**Aspen Mountain**
**My holy grail**
**My daily bread**
**And soup**
**At Bonnie's.**
**Smiling faces**
**Great food**
**Good friends**
**A slice of heaven**
**On a hill.**

**\* \* \* \* \***

## Brother Son

Achievements,
Those worthwhile
Are won in a sprint
Not in a mile
In money
For what it's worth
The gain is fame
For a short time
The longer goal,
The mare, the foal
Yours alone.
My first's a colt
For sure he'll bolt with the best
Put to the test
Himself
Above all others
Strive to win
Please don't give in
Not to me
Nor any other
In spirit my son
Be my brother.

\* \* \* \* \*

# Classical Music

Classical music
Is what I listen to
In my home
Alone
Or with
Special others.
Tartini
Vivaldi
And Revel whose Bolero
Do tell
Has always
Been my favorite
piece
And peace
Is totally
what we all
Seek
'Cept those
Seeking power
To destroy
what all
Enjoy.
Even they
That fall prey
To evil
Need peace.

\* \* \* \* \*

## Clovelly

I grew up
In the culture
Of that time
And place
We all
Start the race
Somewhere
Sydney
In the sixties
Was a sight
To behold
Truth be told,
And I was
In the center
Of that universe
Amongst
The top
Athletes,
Businessmen
And Criminals
Of that time
They were all mates
At a time
When crime
Was King
And the Prince
Was Perce
Norm ran the show
And Clive
Was the greatest
of his time.

* * * * *

# The Coffee Pot

Turn on the switch
The red fire comes burning on,
Heating the small red coffee pot
Slowly, surely
A soft caress, a warming touch
And the blood begins to bubble
And boil in frenzy
A scream of wild joy
A climax of ecstasy
My coffee pot has come
To bring me
The delights of her brew.

* * * * *

# Courageous

The Young
Get strong
The Old
Get bold
The Older
Want
Their story told.
I love my friends
Strong
Old
Bold
Courageous.

\* \* \* \* \*

# Cycling High

Gliding
Through
Time
And space
with
Style
And grace
Searching
For
That special place
Believe
And you will achieve
Nirvana.

\* \* \* \* \*

## Dinner with Mary Jane

One night last winter
I had the pleasure
To dine with Mary Jane
With some good friends
Who had dined with her
On many odd occasions
While I had but watched
From the spy-hole of my mind.
It was a very interesting evening
I tripped with her and them
And perceived much.
I saw the diamonds in the sky
And on the floor
And time drifted slowly by,
Of that I'm sure.
And I remember well
Thoughts of heaven, of hell
Thought vibrations, sound and smell
Defined and pure
Designed to lure
Me back again
And I'll go back, of that I'm sure
To clear the fog; seek, explore
For Mary Jane may hold the key
To a higher form of reality.
But I'll look with caution behind this door
Perhaps Mary Jane's an unclean whore.

\* \* \* \* \*

# Dream

I looked into your eyes
And saw into your heart
Which opened mine
Both eyes and heart
And mind
Wide open
To the possibilities
That come so rarely
In a life
Full of them.
Dream always
Reach for the sky
A falling star
May just fall
Into your arms.

\* \* \* \* \*

# Enough Said

Maroon Bells TT
Aspen Cycling Club
The race of truth
On a hot August night
And truth be told
As always
It was fucking hard
Home now
Kicking back
Had my pot pill
Legal in Colorado
And who gives a fuck
In any case
Surely not me
What will be
will be.
And that race
was fucking hard
My time was slow
But my effort was solid
Which makes it all good
All you can ever do
Is your best.
Truly that's the test
For all
Of all
Be the best
you can be
And in the end
That's enough.

\* \* \* \* \*

# Every Day Remembering Michael Killian

Rode today
Up the way
Up Smuggler
Out my back door
In the sunshine of the day
A way to pray
And remember
Friends of mine
And other days
Gone by
Still asking why
I got to live
And they got to die.
Not sure I'll ever know
Ride on
On trail
And ocean
And snow
Always the way to go
For me
Feel free
And alive
Every day.
Enjoy the gift
Of living
Every day!

\* \* \* \* \*

# Eye to Eye with the Reaper

Today, in Jackson
I looked the Reaper
In the eye
His look

Said
You die!

I saw the tree
meant to kill me
Or break my neck
What the heck
Death looked good
For sure better
Than being a bed wetter

But was not to be
And so I'll ski
Another day or two.
Wouldn't you?

\* \* \* \* \*

# Forever

How to explain
The inexplicable
Better not to try
We live
We die
Is there more
Don't know
For sure
But know enough
To live
The moment
And moments matter
They stay
With us
For a lifetime
Some moments shine
Brightly
in our memories
The finest times
Are buried
Treasures
That sustain us,
Nurture our spirit
In trying times
And joyful moments
In our
Forever

\* \* \* \* \*

# Global Warming

Global warming
Heed the warning
The earth
Is speaking
We should be seeking
Answers
And solutions
To pollutions
Of the very air
That gives life
And breath.

We listen
But don't always hear
of ozone holes
And
Atmosphere
Filthy
From our
Gluttony
And excess.

Time to open
Eyes
And mind
Our
Future.

\* \* \* \* \*

# Gods

Gods
That be
What are they
To me?
Jesus Christ
He walked the earth
For sure
A mortal man
But greater than?
Thor
Or Ra?
Ha Ha Ha
Mohammed
Buddha
All the rest
East is east
west is west
North and South
we know
so little
Thin skinned
And brittle
Children
Of this earth
Are we.
What will be
will be

\* \* \* \* \*

# A Good Day

Was a good day
Was today
Started out
The usual way
Up the hill
Chase the thrill
Racing down
Owning time
A moment
Captured
In your mind.
The finest memories
Captured again
And relived
Now and then
With a friend
Who dared
And cared
Back when

\* \* \* \* \*

# Good Stuff

It's April Tenth
Tani's birthday
And I just told
My daughter Logan
How
Fan-fucking-tastic
The skiing's been
This last week.
Best of all, this season
Of 2015.
Shoulda been
There today
Carvin' corn
On Lift 1A
Noon 'til three
Just me
And a stray dog
Or three
Carving corn
Skier porn
An addiction
An affliction
An elation
Ecstasy
In the warm and wet
Slippery stuff.
Can't get enough
Good stuff!

\* \* \* \* \*

## Hard Iron Doors

I grew up a lot that night I'm sure
when I heard the clang of a metal door
And looked at walls of yellow grey
Stained with vomit, spit, decay
A light that's dim, an acrid smell
Man's own laws, man's own hell
The men around, one a boy
Has this young thief known any joy?
And now to sleep while the dim light burns
A restless night, the stomach churns
Morning comes, a new day's here
In some faces hope, in others fear

I've walked away and now know more
I've opened my mind, my own metal door.

\* \* \* \* \*

# In a Wine Bar

It's dark outside,
But darker within
For within holds the key to life
And life is knowing
And the sound within, is growing—

Loud!
And the people are proud
No – the people are loud
For they do not seek—

And to seek is to know
That the finest sounds are quiet—
The whisper of the wind
The rustle of the leaves
The softness of the snow
The slow easy breath of a child
Sleeping, at peace, in the night
For the child does not know
That it's dark – outside.

\* \* \* \* \*

# Integrity

My teeth chew at my jaw
Cannot stand to draw
And so I sit and write
So many wrongs
I think
I see
A little more
Don't close the door
Walk in and look
Around
Be profound
And search a little
Here and there
Climb up the stair
And look about
Whisper
Please don't shout
The lady she is here
Knowledge is her name
Education is her aim
She fires her arrow true
At him and her and me and you
Who listen
To her message
And what she says to me—
Integrity

\* \* \* \* \*

## Into Tomorrow

**Out tonight**
**Dinner**
**With Logan**
**Justin and Fane**
**The new gal in town**
**Rippin' it up**
**Livin' the dream**
**Stormin' the scene**
**with**
**The Princess of Wild**
**Strutting her style**
**Charging through life**
**Day at a time**
**Children of mine**
**Good hearted souls**
**On their journey**
**Into tomorrow**

\* \* \* \* \*

# Jambalaya

**Jambalaya
Light the fire
Words come out
Softly shout
Freedom's ring
Hear the call
Peace to all
The message
One world
One people
Of many races
Different faces
But the same heart
within
Holds the key
Without which
Poor and Rich
Cannot unite
Barack Obama
'Tis your karma
Lead the way
To a better day
Answer the call
Peace to all.**

**\* \* \* \* \***

# A Jewel

I know a jewel
That shines
Brightly, dully
For me

When it's dull
It looks so hard, and cold
But still so much
A jewel

When it shines
It makes the sun look cold
On a warm day

When it shines
It's like a diamond
In a heap of coal
All can be, but one is

And it's not what it was
Or what it will be
It's what it is

Rough, uncut, used, abused
Warm and tender,
Hard and brutal

But always a jewel

I know why I seek it.

\* \* \* \* \*

# Journey

Journey
Passing our time
Hurtling through space
At a snail pace
In a rat race
For first place
Top the list
For seconds
That count
For nothing
Yet last
Longer than
Your time
Indicates.
Time waits for no one
So linger there
Breathe the air
Of victory
In
That moment.

\* \* \* \* \*

# King Hill

If you race bikes
Then you know
Just how deep
Can you go?
In life
And the pain locker
Lives
Within us all
And so we go
Hard
As hell
Time will tell
How we went
But to strive
Is to live
Well
I'll tell
A tale of hell
On the road To heaven
There is a ride
Just up the way
will test your mettle
And settle
Your mind
Always
leads the way
Be the best
Meet the test
Be the king
Of King Hill
Go hard!

\* \* \* \* \*

# Knock, Knock—Who's There?

And so it's done
Who lost
Who won
Each and every
One and all
Both sides
Losers
Winners
None
Justice done
A dis-service
Did she deserve this
Mockery?
Did we?
I think not
In the end all we've got
Are the rules
We choose to play by
Fair and square
Even Steven
Even though who's got the dough
'S better chance
To finish even.

The good doctor
Fought the law
Called their bluff
Had the stuff
The courage and conviction
To risk it all
Bet his freedom
on a pair of deuces
Right and privacy
'Gainst a black king
Of hypocrisy
And so
Now we know
Tho' the
Hunter prevailed
On this occasion,
Chased the fox
From his doors
Is that someone
Knockin' on yours?

\* \* \* \* \*

# Lazy Sky Flying Man

Walking along the roadway of life
Across the oceans, a day at a time
Carrying all I've got
My clothes, my tools
Of work and pleasure
Both the one

Just a lazy sky flying man

On the run, taking my time
Been there yesterday
Going there tomorrow
Hope I'm here today.

Moving too fast, seeing too much
Moving too slow, same places to go
Can't see it all; seen enough for now
Going to the mountains anyhow

Just a lazy sky flying man.

* * * * *

# Logan's Poem

Logan…
My only
Female child
Something sweet
And something wild
Sweet
Like a tangerine
Wild
Like a wolverine
Such a
Contradiction
Drives her poor dad to
Distraction
Perfect

\* \* \* \* \*

# Lords of the Square

Sitting here, on my deck
In Aspen, Colorado
Half a world away
Listening to Bob Dylan
And his rhyming way
Drifts me back
Across time and waters
To many a great day
At Clovelly Bay

Seems like yesterday
Though more than forty years ago
My life was the ocean—
Had never seen the snow
And I've had full many thrills
In my lifetime I can say
But few can compare
With body surfing from the Square
Into – Clovelly Bay!

**Off the rocks**
**Below the cliffs**
**Waves crashing**
**Arms thrashing**
**Off the Square**

**We sallied forth**
**To surf the Square**
**Or the Far North**
**The Lords of the Square.**

**Harry and Donny led the way**
**And Chubby always had a say**
**The Hardies, Ron and George, were there**
**with Zeke and Monkey, Brigga, Dave, and Hobber.**
**Duffy, Thin, Grouper, and Frenchy, too.**

**Me, I rounded out our crew,**
**Those Lords of the Square.**

**\* \* \* \***

## Merchants of Doubt

Climate Science
Deniers
Charlatans
Thieves and liars
Sowing the seeds
Of doubt
About
The future
Of humanity
Soul-less ghouls
They break the rules
Of civilized conduct
Merchants of Doubt
and destruction
Destroying the planet
with avarice
And greed.
The same cabal
Of evil
That lobbied
For deadly cigarettes
Is the same
that poison minds
with climate science
Denial
Vile
Contemptible
Vermin

\* \* \* \* \*

# A Mountain

It's dark outside
But the mountain's white
Glowing in the dark
Ominous, foreboding, vast
And the mountain breathes
Cold and white
Soft and light
Powder;
Tomorrow, perhaps the sun will shine
And the virgin will be pure, and mine
To caress;
Softly
In the trees, so quiet.
I live to love

The softness
Of nature, and the snow.

\* \* \* \* \*

# My Holy Place

I have
A special place
A holy place
To go to.

My favorite sports
Skiing and cycling
Give easiest access
To this portal
This special vacuum
In time
And space.

Going fast
On skis
Or the bike
Allows me
To enter
a vacuum
Of focus
And tranquility

A holy place
For me

* * * * *

# Of Death and Dying

Most fear death
Though 'tis certain
More so than tomorrow
Than life
We fear the unknown
And death is surely this
Finally, life's farewell kiss
A kiss to wonder at
To know but once.
Perhaps
A soft caress
A frightened scream
A silent nod
A lingering dream
Of tranquility.

\* \* \* \* \*

# Old World People

Europe, I've looked at you with some of my soul
And come to understand some of your mould
From the dimness of gray lights, gray bars, cold
Through a simple woman, with heart of gold

With bread, to begin the day
Different words, the same things to say

Old ways, rich in history
Deep dark eyes, pillars of mystery

Tradition, a wealth of cultures
Made strong by eagles, ravished by vultures.

Centuries of struggle; good times, bad
Simple folk; strong, warm, happy, sad

Joyous in the living of each day

Walking through life in their old world way.

\* \* \* \* \*

# Owning

**Philosophy**
**Not a substance**
**Intangible**
**Still something**
**That can be owned.**
**Unlike all the rest**
**Feelings are**
**The only thing**
**We ever own.**

**\* \* \* \* \***

# Passion

**Passion
When she
Comes forth
I am her slave
There is no escape
No excuse
No respite
From her
Torments.
And no regrets
of running
With her
And my
Will
For in the end
Passion
Drives us
Harder
Faster
And more gently
Forward
Always
Urging us
To never
Ever
Give in
To less
Than what
She
Gives us**

* * * * *

## Passion and Harmony

If you don't have
Passion
and
Harmony
in your life,
you have
Little
Things
That don't
Mean
Much.

* * * * *

# Poem for All Seasons

"God's children"
**Kill**
Mostly one another
Brother against brother
Child against her father
Abused by the same
Some people are insane
Driven by a God
Of their choice
His voice
Goes unheard
By the herd
Shouting his name
In defiance
Of what is right.
The Moral Compass
Steers through
A night of darkness
And despair
Time will tell
Heaven or hell
On earth.

\* \* \* \* \*

# Port Wine

The whole thing
Drank it all
Yet didn't crawl
Away.
Bottle of port
Drained it dry
Didn't try
To drink the other
Lord knows why
Some nights I'd try
And I believe
Succeed.
Hollow victory
Drunken hero
Biggest winner
Loses most tomorrow.
Have no sorrow
For the victim
Of indulgence.
Victory hangs over him.
Porcelyn's Memorial Grail
Is within his grasp
Embraced and kissed
spat, spewed and pissed
Upon, with feeling
The drunk is reeling
Away
Did you hear him say
Tomorrow is another day.

* * * * *

# A Raven

I saw a raven
In the sky
Flying low
Close to the ground
Floating down
That line
by Lift Six
Where I remember
him, Hansi,
Skiing so well
Master
of his craft
Soaring
His spirit
Flying
Floating
in the sky
I saw
A raven

* * * * *

## Sanity

The war on drugs
Fought, in the streets
Defeats, all reason
Treason
By the nation's leaders
Of the people.
For self
Not same
Insane aim
Without direction
Deaf, unhearing
Steering
Towards destruction
Of free will
And in turn
Those freedoms
That were earned
By sweat and work
And desire
Will light the fires
Of insurrection.
Resurrection
And perhaps
Sanity
Will overcome vanity.

\* \* \* \* \*

# Satisfaction

**Satisfaction**
**The Holy Grail**
**Of desire**
**Fulfilled.**
**Obtainable**
**But unsustainable**
**A fleeting thing**
**Lingering**
**Only briefly**
**Memorable**
**But Immeasurable**
**In the sands**
**Of time**
**That is**
**A life.**

**\* \* \* \* \***

# Science Rules

Science
Is, by
Definition.
Analysis
And Assessment
Of fact
Fact is
we're all fucked
without
The fucking facts
Analyzed
By the brightest minds
And the signs
Say
The smartest minds
Are scientists
Not fuckwits
As so many
Politicians
Seem to be
It's time to be
Revolutionary
For our time
And all time
And say
Every day
Science rules!

School the fools
Science rules!

\* \* \* \* \*

# The Seeker

I once asked of a seeker
Seeker
Where do you go
What will you find
What is love
What is lust
Who is God
Is it you
Is there truth
What is truth
Is there reason
Or logic

Seeker
Why do you go
Do you know

Said the Seeker

What will I find.

\* \* \* \* \*

# Short Thought Medley One

We are but
Shards of light
In the sands
Of time.

Good health
Is the ultimate
Success.

Memories
And the moment
Are
All there really is.

You just need
Enough
Not
A lot.

Your life
Is a day long
Every day.

Never hesitate
To contemplate
Too late!

Poetry:
To say as much as I can
With as few words as possible.

\* \* \* \* \*

# Short Thought Medley Two

Eagles swoop
Sparrows fly
A life to live
A way to die.

Life is a slow process
Security is the ultimate escape.

Living is the ultimate experience
Of which love is but a part
Knowledge is a broken heart.

In this sea of people
Some great wave
Threw us together
A fishhook to a seagull.

You can't change the thinking
Of an educated man
Only an intelligent one.

To be in harmony
Is
To be in time
With
Nature's heartbeat.

Better to say nothing
Than to try to say it all.

* * * * *

# Sinaro

S I N A R O, Sinaro
Spiritual Individual
Not A Religious One
This is my creed
My son calls me
Ironically
The High Priest
Of Sinaro.
We are all on
A spiritual journey
Our humanity
Lives within us all
Answer the call
Peace to all

\* \* \* \* \*

# Skugly Skagro

Skiing is my passion
It gives my life
Meaning
And direction
and has shaped my life
Every turn I make
Is a reflection
Of the direction
I have chosen
And is, in essence
A noble choice
It gives voice
To my emotion


Anderl Molterer
One of the greatest skiers
To ever live among us
Gave me my favorite
Skiing complement
So many years ago:
"When you ski aggressively,
you ski very, very well."

Ski ugly
Ski aggressively

"Skugly Skagro"

My skiing mantra
I utter it
At the start
Of almost every run
Every turn
Matters
On the hill
And in life

Attack!

Skugly Skagro!

\* \* \* \* \*

# Spirit of Humanity

Organized religion
Not for me
Rather the spirit
Of humanity
Truth to all
Universally
Undivided
By nation,
Creed,
Or intolerance.
Truth
Speaks one language
Common to all
Uncommon
To greed
Corruption,
And indifference
To the human spirit
That lies within
All that are
The truly Human
Beings
That we are

\* \* \* \* \*

# Take Your Time

Diet
Exercise
And sleep
Divine trinity
Of good health
The greatest wealth
Free to all
All for free
Time
The only price
To pay
Time
Waits
For no one
So take whatever
Today
And your body
give you
Enjoy your time
After all
That's all
There is.

\* \* \* \* \*

## Ted

Met him
Daytime
In a bar
His reputation
Went far
Back in time
Beer cost a dime
And you fought
For your belief
In the street
It was neat
Then
Men were men
Not paper tigers
Wimps and liars
Didn't last
A whole long while
For men
Were men
Then
Had Style
Honour
And integrity
Way to be
Then.
And now
Aren't too many
Don't take shit
A pity
Ain't it!

\* \* \* \* \*

# Tenacity

**Tenacity**
**The word**
**Rolls off the tongue**
**With a bite**
**Of conviction**
**A taste**
**of perseverity.**
**What a wonderful**
**Quality**
**To have**
**In that arsenal**
**Of characteristics**
**That give us**
**Personality**

\* \* \* \* \*

# A Thinker

A thinker doesn't think
As such
He watches, learns, observes
Applies
His touch.
For to touch is to feel,
And to feel is to think
So very many people reach this brink
But they do not plunge
deep, within their mind
A thinker dives – deep
Some don't come up
Just wander in their sleep
But he who dives
To his deepest depth
And rises to the surface, out of breath
Has learned
That life is to think.

\* \* \* \* \*

# This Moment

Stay in each moment
As long as possible
At that time
And understand
That wisdom lives
in the moment.
Depression
Lives in the past.
Anxiety flourishes
With thoughts of the future
Happiness
And wisdom
Are alive
And thrive
in
This moment

* * * * *

# Three Legged Dog

I am an old man
Have had a great run
In the great game
Of life
Grew up
In the school
Of hard knocks
In the streets
The surf
And on the pitch
And paid the price.
I ache
Not for the old days
But because of them.
Knees and shoulders mostly
But all over generally
I ache
Still, you've got to laugh
As my daughter and I did
A few nights back
When I told her
How hard it is
To get up
Off the floor
After working out.
Still, just like a three legged dog,
Find a way
Through every day
Live a life
And laugh

\* \* \* \* \*

# To Ski

**Lay the blade**
**Carve the turn**
**Accelerate**
**Exhilarate**
**Controlled speed**
**Flowing motion**
**Racing**
**Down the mountain**
**Desperately**
**Senses reeling**
**A special feeling**

**To live, to be**

**To ski**

**\* \* \* \* \***

# Wisdom

My mind
Twisted
Not warped
Different

For sure
Not rich
Not poor
Still with much wealth
Seeking more
Greedy
Lustful
Give me all

Every bit
The soul
The wit
The dirt
The shit
Spew

From the floor
The gut
The gore
Give me more
*WISDOM*

\* \* \* \* \*

# About the Poet

Ed Cross grew up in the Eastern Suburbs of Sydney, Australia. After a 1965 ski trip to Thredbo, his passion for skiing eventually led him to Aspen, Colorado.

He worked for the Aspen Mountain Ski Patrol from 1971 to 1988.

Ed began writing poetry in 1971, and credits the Aspen Poets Society with his renewed interest in writing new poems and cataloging his early poems.

His poetry has been included in *The Ski Book* and in Hunter Thompson's *Kingdom of Fear*. He has also submitted many of his poems to Aspen newspapers.

Ed is the proud father of Tyson, Justin, and Logan.

\* \* \* \* \*